CANADA

The Introduction of Christianity
in Early Canada

STEVEN R. MARTINS

*Dedicated to my four children,
Matthias, Timothy, Nehemias, and Raquel*

cantaroinstitute.org

Canada: The Introduction of Christianity in Early Canada by Steven R. Martins.

Published by Cántaro Publications, a publishing imprint of the Cántaro Institute, Jordan Station, ON.

© 2020, 2025 by Cántaro Institute. All rights reserved. Except for brief quotations in critical publications or reviews, no part of this book may be reproduced in any manner without prior written consent from the publishers.

Unless otherwise indicated, Scripture quotations are from the ESV® Bible (The Holy Bible, English Standard Version®). Copyright © 2001 by Crossway, a publishing ministry of Good News Publishers. Used by permission. All rights reserved.

Book design by Cántaro Publications.

Library & Archives Canada

ISBN 978-1-7772356-6-6

Printed in the United States

ABOUT THE CÁNTARO INSTITUTE
Inheriting, Informing, Inspiring

Cántaro Institute is a reformed evangelical organization committed to the advancement of the Christian worldview for the reformation and renewal of the church and culture.

We believe that as the Christian church returns to the fount of Scripture as her ultimate authority for all knowing and living, and wisely applies God's truth to every aspect of life, her missiological activity will result in not only the renewal of the human person but also the reformation of culture, an inevitable result when the true scope and nature of the gospel is made known and applied.

CONTENTS

CANADA
The Introduction of
Christianity in Early Canada   9
    A Christian Canada?   9
    The Earlier Explorers   11
    John Cabot   12
    Jacques Cartier   16
    Samuel de Champlain   22
    Later Missionaries   28
    Christian Influence & the Reformation 36
    The Major Denominations of
    Pre-Confederation   41
    In Summary   48

APPENDIX
The Peace Tower, Parliament,
and Christian Canada   51
    The Peace Tower   55
    Parliament Buildings   59
    Memorial Chamber   61
    Concluding Remarks   63

About the Author   65

CANADA

THE INTRODUCTION OF CHRISTIANITY IN EARLY CANADA

A Christian Canada?

WAS THERE EVER A "Christian" Canada? That depends on how we might interpret the term. Do we mean a predominant *Christian* consensus at some point in our Canadian history? Or a nation that exhibited a culture and society that aligned with the teachings of God's Word? It was certainly more "Christian" than the United States of America, in terms of its orthodoxy that is, and that is, unashamedly, coming from an American historian, Mark L. Noll.[1] Irregardless as to what you might believe on the

---

1. Mark A. Noll, *What Happened to Christian Canada?* (Vancouver: Regent College Publishing, 2007), 7-9.

matter – as to whether a "Christian" Canada has *ever* existed – what *can* be said with certainty is that the Christian faith had a significant influence on Canada's early national development.

Consider, for example, that the Christian faith was first introduced to what would later be called "the Great White North" by the early explorers John Cabot (c. 1450-1500), Jacques Cartier (1491-1557), Samuel de Champlain (1574-1635), and later European missionaries. Although the faith was predominantly Roman Catholic at the time of its arrival, given that the Protestant Reformation had not officially started until 1517 with Luther's *Ninety-Five Theses*, the early work of the Récollets and Jesuit missionaries helped open the door, ironically considering its later hostility, for the later *reformed* faith to plant itself in Canada. If we hope to understand Christianity's influence on Canadian society and culture, prior to Canadian Confederation, we need to have an understanding of the Christian faith's introduction in New France and the Northern British colonies. Because irregardless of what secular historians might claim, as may be evident by the increasing historical revisionism in academia today, Canada, as a nation, does in fact have historic *Christian* roots.

The Early Explorers

The first discovery of the Americas was initially by the Norse in AD 986, but permanent settlement was never realized, partly as a result of violent skirmishes between the Norse and the First Nations. However, in 1492, the Americas were once again discovered by Christopher Columbus, who originally thought he had arrived in India, and thus called the Caribbean the "West Indies."[2] The pursuit of the northwest passage immediately became a frenzy for colonizing the new world, largely because of the gold and gems that were discovered by the Spanish in Central and South America. Though the French and the British made attempts to colonize various parts of the Americas, it was the venetian John Cabot who first discovered North America on behalf of Britain, and ahead of France, in the late 1400s.

---

2. R. Douglas Francis, Richard Jones, and Donald B. Smith, eds., *Origins: Canadian History to Confederation*, sixth edition (Toronto: Nelson Education, 2009), 25-28.

John Cabot

Cabot was granted authority in the month of March 1496, by King Henry VII of Britain, to sail all parts of "the eastern, western and northern seas."[3] As the patent reads:

> Under our banners, flags and ensigns, with five ships or vessels of whatsoever burden and quantity they may be... to find, discover and investigate whatsoever islands, countries, regions or provinces of heathens and infidels, in whatsoever part of the world placed, which before this time were unknown to all Christians.[4]

What Cabot discovered and would later claim as British land was the east coast of Newfoundland, but his expedition was relatively short compared to other explorers.[5] He was only

---

3. Douglas Hunter, *The Race to the New World: Christopher Columbus, John Cabot, and a Lost History of Discovery* (New York, NY.: Palgrave Macmillan, 2011), 165.
4. *Patent granted by King Henry VII to John Cabot*, Heritage Newfoundland & Labrador, accessed February 25, 2016, http://www.heritage.nf.ca/articles/exploration/1496-cabot-patent.php/.
5. Francis et al., eds., *Origins: Canadian History to*

willing to go ashore with his crew once, and only willing to travel a crossbow-shot's distance.[6]

Pinpointing exactly *where* Cabot landed has proven difficult, as the twentieth century historian Henry Harrisse attested:

> The documents of the time, geographic and historical, which have come down to us, fail to mention the locality of John Cabot's landfall in his first transatlantic voyage. We can only presume, but with great probability, that it was on some point of the north-east coast of Labrador.[7]

Details are also scarce as to whether Cabot brought along religious leaders for his voyage, or whether they accompanied him on land in 1497. If he did, which has been the general assumption, they would have clearly been Roman Catholic, given that Britain had yet to break with Rome.[8]

Confederation, 29.
6. Hunter, *The Race to the New World*, 189.
7. Henry Harrisse, *John Cabot the Discoverer of North America and Sebastian His Son* (New York, NY.: Argosy-Antiquarian, 1968 [orig. 1896]), 69.
8. Douglas J. Wilson, *The Church Grows in Canada* (Toronto: The Ryerson Press, 1966), 18.

CANADA

With the lack of detailed information, we can only assume that Cabot's planting of a Christian cross, along with the planting of British and Venetian banners, was with the intention of declaring the land as Christian, since it was claimed under the authority of the British king.[9] This cross would have served as the first introduction of the Christian faith to North America, considering that indigenous tribes inhabited Newfoundland at the time, however, it certainly would not have served as an effective gospel symbol for the natives, given that the cross, without the context of the gospel message, would only have been perceived as two pieces of wood nailed together. This was, nonetheless, only the beginning.[10]

Between John Cabot and Jacques Cartier, there were two other travellers who arrived on Canadian shores, the first was Gaspar Corte-Real, an Azorean commissioned by the Portuguese, who arrived somewhere in Newfoundland. It is not clear whether there was any proclamation

---

9. Francis et al., eds., *Origins: Canadian History to Confederation*, 29.
10. Hunter, *The Race to the New World*, 189.

of the gospel, but similar to Cabot, it was the Portuguese custom to raise a cross on newly discovered land.[11] What is recorded against his witness, however, is the kidnapping of fifty-seven First Nations who were sent off to Europe. Their story remains a mystery, but the fate of Corte-Real and his crew is reported to have been a tragic loss at sea.[12]

The second explorer after Corte-Real was Giovanni de Verrazzano, an Italian navigator under the commission of France. As opposed to Corte-Real, Verrazzano did not have much interaction, if at all, with the natives of North America, instead prioritizing the cartography of the Carolinas up to Gaspé. But neither Corte-Real, who claimed Canada for Portugal, and Verrazzano, were successful in settling the North American continent, and not much is known as to whether they testified of the Christian faith. Although, if Corte-Real had done so in his interactions with the First Nations, it would not have

---

11. H.A. Tanser, *Westward to the Americas* (Toronto: Longmans Canada Limited, 1967 [orig. 1954]), 8-9.
12. Francis et al., eds., *Origins: Canadian History to Confederation*, 30.

been positively received due to his abduction of the fifty-seven natives, a clear disregard of their human dignity, and an act contrary to Christian teaching.[13]

Jacques Cartier

After Corte-Real and Verrazano, the French commissioned a wealthy Frenchman, Jacques Cartier, from the port of Saint-Malo, northwestern France, to succeed Verrazzano's quest for the northwest passage to the eastern world.[14] He is believed to have arrived at Belle Isle, between Labrador and Newfoundland, in May 1534, and later the Gulf of St. Lawrence, where he landed in Prince Edward Island. His journey from there into Quebec resulted in encounters with the Mi'kmaq and the Iroquois, both of whom developed friendships with Cartier for the purpose of trade.[15]

Cartier's experience with the indigenous led him to believe that they were an easy people to convert, mainly because of their simplicity of living, however he did not find it appropriate

---

13. Ibid., 30-31.
14. Ibid., 31.
15. Ibid.

to carry out a full-fledged missionary campaign without the necessary churchmen to do so.[16] Cartier explains that they did nonetheless testify of the gospel, in what way they could, without a proper translator, writing:

> On [Friday] the twenty-fourth of the said month [July], we had a cross made thirty feet high, which was put together in the presence of a number of [First Nations] on the point at the entrance to this harbor... We erected this cross on the point in their presence and they watched it being put together and set up. And when it had been raised in the air, we all knelt down with our hands joined, worshiping it before them; and made signs to them, looking up and pointing towards heaven, that by means of this we had our redemption, at which they showed many marks of admiration, at the same time turning and looking at the cross.[17]

Unfortunately, the image Carter left was not the true Christian faith, but rather a deformation

---

16. Jacques Cartier, *The Voyages of Jacques Cartier*, ed. Ramsay Cook (Toronto: University of Toronto Press, 1993 [orig. 1924]), 22.
17. Ibid., 26.

Figure 1: "Cartier Erecting a Cross at Gaspe" by Charles W. Jefferys, 1934. From *Canada's Past in Pictures* (Toronto, Ryerson, 1934), p. 12. Library and Archives Canada, Acc. No. 1996-282-1.

of Christianity, portraying an idolatrous faith where the cross is worshiped instead of the one who was on the cross, but the traditional Catholic defense may be made here to identify the cross as an icon, which has been a controversial subject between Catholics and Protestants as to whether a revered icon should be considered an idol.

The twentieth century scholar, Douglas J. Wilson of the University of Toronto, commented that Cartier's motives were more earthly-oriented than divine, that is to say, he had in mind the interests of "the city of man" rather than the "City of God." This is because all six crosses that he had erected, "notably the ones at Gaspé and Montreal," bore the "*fleur de lis* and the name of his French king."[18] It would be an unfair assessment, however, to suggest that Cartier was uncatholic in his vision for what would be New France, as Wilson seems to suggest in his dismissal of Cartier's cross-raising as merely superficial.[19] His priority, as commissioned by the king, was to claim new

---

18. Wilson, *The Church Grows in Canada*, 1.
19. Ibid.

territory for France, and the religion of France was Roman Catholicism, so it follows that the crosses were not only to mark French territory but to declare such territory as Catholic, the official state religion.

Contrary to Wilson's perspective, Cartier in fact demonstrates a concern for the spiritual condition of the First Nations, writing:

> I, in my simple understanding, and without being able to give any other reason, am of opinion that it pleases God in His divine goodness that all human beings inhabiting the surface of the globe, just as they have sight and knowledge of the sun, have had and are to have in time to come knowledge of and belief in our holy faith.[20]

This thus implied being more intentional in proclaiming the gospel, which Cartier did on his second journey, speaking, with the help of a translator, on the idolatrous worship of the Iroquois.[21] He recounts this interaction in his writings:

---

20. Cartier, *The Voyages of Jacques Cartier*, 37.
21. John W. Grant, *Moon of Wintertime: Missionaries and the Indians of Canada in Encounter Since 1534* (Toronto: University of Toronto Press, 1984), 3.

> We showed them their error and informed them that their *Cudouagny* was a wicked spirit who deceived them, and there is but one God, Who is in Heaven, Who gives us everything we need and is the Creator of all things and that in Him alone we should believe... several other points concerning our faith were explained to them which they believed without trouble, and... several times they begged the Captain to cause them to be baptized."[22]

However, similar to the Portuguese, Cartier likewise violated the principles of the Christian faith by kidnapping the Iroquoian chief's sons, whom he later returned after visiting France, and abducting ten natives whom he never returned to Canada again.[23] Although the gospel had been more explicitly proclaimed amongst the Iroquois, the actions of the explorer once again betrayed his message, but the seeds were sown for a future opportunity that would be realized by Samuel de Champlain in the early 1600s.

---

22. Cartier, *The Voyages of Jacques Cartier*, 68.
23. Francis et al., eds., *Origins: Canadian History to Confederation*, 31-32.

Samuel de Champlain

Champlain first arrived in the new world as a cartographer under François Gravé du Pont, who sailed up the St. Lawrence river in 1603. A year later, he accompanied Pierre Dugua de Mons to Acadia, and was tasked with acting as a diplomat in dealings with the First Nations. It was later in 1608, however, that Champlain was sent by Dugua de Mons "to establish a settlement at Quebec, where the fur trade with native peoples in the interior could be controlled more easily."[24]

Champlain is believed to have been baptized as a Protestant, but later became a Catholic sometime prior to his transatlantic journey.[25] His missionary zeal is exhibited in his encounters with the indigenous, in which he taught "the grand Sagamo" of the Mi'kmaq that "there was but one God who made all things in heaven

---

24. Marcel Trudel and Mathieu D'Avignon, "Samuel de Champlain," The Canadian Encyclopedia, August 29, 2013, accessed June 13, 2016, http://www.thecanadianencyclopedia.ca/en/article/samuel-de-champlain/.
25. Ibid.

and earth."²⁶ When witnessing the First Nations without the Christian faith or law, living without God, he was convicted that "I should be committing a grave sin if I did not make it my business to devise some means of bringing them to the knowledge of God."²⁷

This led Champlain to teach the First Nations of the truth of the Gospel, commencing with the creation narrative. He explained that God fashioned Adam from the earth, and that from his rib God made Eve, and that the God who created them, and the God whom they worshiped, was not the four gods as the Mi'kmaq believed, but one God in three persons. In fact, according to historians Conrad Heidenreich and Janet Ritch, when Chaplain mentions the doctrine of the Trinity:

> Champlain is citing the Apostles' Creed here, which adds the descent into hell to the other articles of faith found in the Nicene Creed: that

---

26. Samuel de Champlain, *Voyages to New France* (Toronto: Oberon Press, 1972), 72.
27. Raymonde Litalien and Denis Vaugeois, eds., *Champlain: The Birth of French America* (Montreal & Kingston: McGill-Queen's University Press, 2004), 198.

Jesus was conceived by the power of the Holy Spirit, born of the Virgin Mary, suffered death and was buried, rose again, and ascended into the right hand of God the Father.[28]

As Champlain wrote in his *Des Sauvages*:

I asked [the great Sagamo] if he had ever heard that God Himself had come into the world, and he said that he himself had never seen Him... I told him that God had so loved the world that He had given His only begotten Son, conceived by the Holy Ghost and born of the Virgin Mary. His Son, I told him, had lived on earth for thirty-three years, working countless miracles, raising the dead, healing the sick, casting out devils, opening the eyes of the blind, making known the will of His Father, to the end that we might worship and adore Him. I explained that He had shed His blood and suffered Himself to be put to death for us and for our sins, that He had risen on the third day, descended into hell

---

28. Conrad E. Heidenreich and K. Janet Ritch, eds., *Samuel de Champlain Before 1604: Des Sauvages and Other Documents Related to the Period* (Toronto: The Champlain Society, 2010), 279.

and ascended into heaven, where He is seated on the right hand of God the Father.[29]

He sincerely believed that if the country were settled, the First Nations would "readily enough become good Christians and would be the better for it."[30]

Champlain was never characterized as a man without principles, one who would seek after power and riches at the expense of others, or through the exploitation of minorities. On the contrary, as Canadian historian John W. Grant writes:

> Samuel de Champlain, one of the founders of Acadia, was not content to regard the new world merely as a source of quick profits. He conceived the vision of a new society, French in culture and Christian in religion, whose population would consist of converted Indians leavened with French colonists.[31]

He is regarded as a French nobleman, following the example "of the king in the substance of

---

29. Champlain, *Voyages to New France*, 73-75.
30. Ibid., 76.
31. Grant, *Moon of Wintertime*, 6.

his Christian beliefs... men of deep and abiding personal faith, and [having] cultivated a spirit of Christian piety."[32]

Part of the French vision of New France involved sending prisoners, both men and women, to populate the country, a second chance at life, "to live as subjects and in the fear of God in the Apostolic and Roman Catholic Religion," to upstart business with the First Nations people "in every peaceful fashion, to attract and attempt to instruct and lead them to acquaintance with God and His Christian faith."[33] Both the French King and the explorer Champlain "believed that the observance of religion (Christianity) was vital to the stability of society and the state," a foundation for France and what would be Quebec.[34]

It was an admirable vision, an aspiring dream, however, the mistake that he, along with many others, made was attempting to make the

---

32. David Hackett Fischer, *Champlain's Dream* (New York, NY.: Alfred A. Knopf Canada, 2008), 56.
33. Alfred Ramé, ed., «Letters from Henry III, 12 Jan. 1588,» in *Documents inédites sur le Canada. Deuxième Série* (Paris, 1865), 34-44.
34. Fischer, *Champlain's Dream*, 57.

indigenous conform to "French" culture, rather than allow the locals to develop their own culture under the Christian religion.[35] Culture is defined as religion externalized, it is the faith or religion of the people reflected through their cultivation of God's creation into a civilization. It is, as per Christian thinker Andrew Sandlin:

> Those products of human interactivity with nature that reflect the self-conscious goal of human benefit: education, science, entertainment, technology, architecture, the arts – even such simple human products as meals, toys, and personal grooming products.[36]

Thus to refer to "French" culture, as Champlain did, was not only to refer to the Christian faith, but the customs, values, and languages that made Frenchmen French.

The Iroquois, the Algonquin, the Mi'kmaq, and various other First Nations could well have developed a Christian culture had they converted to Christianity, but its society would

---

35. Grant, *Moon of Wintertime*, 14.
36. P. Andrew Sandlin, *Christian Culture: An Introduction* (Mount Hermon, CA.: Center for Cultural Leadership, 2013), 21.

have looked different from the French. The mistake, therefore, was attempting to make the indigenous French, as opposed to allowing both communities to develop a multi-ethnic society under the unifying Christian faith; which is what the Jesuits attempted, allowing "some of its members to adapt Christian practice to the circumstances of other cultures."[37]

Later Missionaries

Cabot's first arrival on Canadian soil may not have commenced with missional enterprise, nor did Cartier's arrival initially launch a large scale missionary campaign amongst the First Nations, given that "the Island of Montreal, for instance, dealt in furs long before it turned to evangelism" and that "religious (Christian) and humanitarian goals in Canadian life were not initially present," but their discoveries paved the way for Champlain to introduce various missionaries, starting first with the Récollets and the later Jesuits.[38]

---

37. Grant, *Moon of Wintertime*, 11.
38. Wilson, *The Church Grows in Canada*, 3-4.

In 1615, three Récollets priests arrived in Quebec to "carve up their vast mission field with heroic optimism," with one covering the "St. Lawrence from Trois-Rivieres to a point somewhat below Quebec," the other covering "Tadoussac to look after the Montagnais of the Saguenay region," and the third traveling a thousand kilometres to "the Georgian Bay to carry the message to the Hurons."[39] In the end, their missions were not successful, failing to provide long-lasting fruit given their "lack of resources to cope with the logistic problems of a transatlantic mission [and] to comply with Indian patterns of mutual present-giving."[40] However, they nonetheless tilled the ground for later Catholic and Protestant missionaries.

A valuable collection of annual reports from the Jesuit missionaries is *The Relations*, which covers forty years of early colonial missions-work in Canada. In these reports, a notable missionary is featured who left his mark on Canadian history, as Wilson states: "Father Jean Brébeuf became famous... his first report in 1635

---

39. Grant, *Moon of Wintertime*, 7.
40. Ibid., 8.

aroused so much interest in France that six other missionaries were sent to help at the Huron mission of Ihonatiria, or St. Joseph."[41]

Brébeuf is regarded as the giant of the Huron missions, a martyr for the Christian faith in early Canada. In his missions work he "composed the first dictionary and grammar of the Huron language, translated prayers into Huron, and wrote the *Huron Carol* in an attempt to give an indigenous interpretation of the nativity."[42] The Huron were perceived as a stronghold of paganism, hence why Brébeuf made it his missionfield, but he ministered in a time where the First Nations often responded with hostility against the French settlers. Any tragedy, whether fire, natural catastrophe, or an epidemic, was perceived to be the fault of the French, and thus the blame fell on God's messengers. When writing to the priests in France, Brébeuf writes:

> Your life hangs by a thread. Of calamities you are the cause – the scarcity of game, a fire,

---

41. Wilson, *The Church Grows in Canada*, 5.
42. Michael D. Clarke, ed., *Canada: Portraits of Faith* (Medicine Hat, AB.: Home School Legal Defence Association of Canada, 2001), 17.

famine, or an epidemic... you are the reasons, and at any time a savage may burn your cabin down or split your head... "Wherein the gain," you may ask? There is no gain but this – that what you suffer shall be of God. So if despite these trials you are ready to share our labours, come; for you will find a consolation in the cross that far outweighs its burdens.[43]

Brébeuf was captured by the Iroquois, enemies of the Huron, and was stripped naked, tortured and burned alive. In all his suffering, he never ceased to preach the gospel, hoping and praying for the repentance and salvation of his captors. His death is described as "the most atrocious martyrdoms in the annals of Christianity," a victim of cannibalism; but throughout his ministry, "his desire was to die for Jesus Christ."[44]

It was a common struggle for the colonial missionaries to witness to the First Nations, not because they were opposed to dialogue, but because they preferred their religious traditions. This inevitably led to a surprising partnership

---
43. Cited in Ibid.
44. Ibid.

between the Catholics and the Protestants at a time when tensions were easing, as both communities temporarily put aside their differences for the advancement of the gospel. This was evident in the Canadian Jesuit, Gabriel Druilettes, visiting the protestant John Eliot of New England in 1650, a missionary who had "mastered several dialects and had invented an Indian alphabet in which he published the Lord's Prayer, the Decalogue and ultimately, the Old and New Testaments," to discuss the difficulties of winning over their indigenous neighbors to the gospel.[45]

It is believed that New England's Protestantism had had a positive effect on the missions work in Canada, influencing the efforts of the Jesuit missionaries, and fostering an openness to partnering with Protestants in New France. However, when New England later decided to annihilate the indigenous (post-King Philip's War in 1675-1676), New France instead encouraged peaceful relations with the First

---

45. Wilson, *The Church Grows in Canada*, 7.

Nations, "exceeding in Christian charity" when compared to the South, as Wilson puts it.[46]

The early years proved difficult for French missionaries, who found great difficulty to explain the gospel in its simplicity, as Grant writes: "Such terms as 'sin,' 'grace,' and 'faith,' which derived their meaning from one [worldview], were not easily comprehended by those accustomed to the other [worldview]."[47] But they were not working with a people who had no plain knowledge of God, as Paul writes in Romans 1:19-20:

> For what can be known about God is plain to them, because God has shown it to them. For his invisible attributes, namely, his eternal power and divine nature, have been clearly perceived, ever since the creation of the world, in the things that have been made. So they are without excuse.

The New Testament scholar Colin G. Kruse writes that this plain reading – that all mankind has a level of knowledge of God – was the

---

46. Ibid., 7-8.
47. Grant, *Moon of Wintertime*, 24.

common interpretation of the early church,[48] citing in his commentary St. Chrysostom, "For what will the [heathen] say in that day? That 'we were ignorant of Thee?'"[49]

This knowledge is made evident in the research of twentieth century ethnologist Wilhelm Schmidt, who discovered that the most primitive civilizations exhibited vestiges of original monotheism, belief in a personal God, referred to with masculine grammar, abiding in the heavens, infinitely superior to man, Creator of all things, moral-law giver and judge of all.[50] As Champlain had concluded: "[The] Indians worshiped one Great Spirit, believed in the immortality of the soul, and had an idea of the Devil. But he regarded them as a people who

---

48. Colin G. Kruse, *Paul's Letter to the Romans*, ed. D.A. Carson, The Pillar New Testament Commentary, (Grand Rapids, MI.: William B. Eerdmans Publishing Company, 2012), 91.
49. 'Homilies on Romans 3' [ACCSR, 39], as cited in Colin G. Kruse, *Paul's Letter to the Romans*, 91.
50. Winfried Corduan, *Neighboring Faiths,* second edition (Illinois: InterVarsity Press, 2012), 32-33.; See Wilhelm Schmidt, *The Origin and Growth of Religion* (Proctorville, OH: Wythe-North Publishing, 2014).

had never been brought to the true faith." It was, then, not a venture of preaching the gospel to a people with no concept of a higher being, but rather, overcoming the language barriers between the French and the indigenous, and confronting the moral rebellion within their own hearts (Rom. 1:18).

It is not until 1749 that Protestant missions formally began to the First Nations, shortly after the founding of Halifax, where, for example, Thomas Wood, a missionary from New Jersey, visited "various Indian encampments during his tenure... from 1753 until his death in 1758... [conducting] services in Mi'kmaq."[51] In Upper Canada, the first indigenous Christian communities emerged as a result of missions work and "the migration of groups already Christian," where Protestant First Nations arrived in Canada "for reasons having to do more directly with religion."[52] As Grant writes of the nineteenth century spike in missionary zeal:

> By the early years of the nineteenth century missionary effort was no longer a preserve of

---
51. Grant, *Moon of Wintertime*, 71.
52. Ibid., 72-73.

pious coteries but was beginning to command widespread support. Heightened sympathy for missions was an after effect of a series of evangelical revivals that concurrently swept the British Isles and the American colonies during the eighteenth century.[53]

Christian Influence & the Reformation

Although what had been first introduced to Canada was a "deformation" of Christianity, in the form of Catholic doctrine, the effects of the Protestant reformation eventually spilled over into the new world, beginning with the Huguenots in Canada, who "originated in 1560." The title "Huguenot" is generally applied "to the Reform or Calvinistic French Protestants" who formed a minority in New France under Champlain.[54] They, being traders and merchants, perceived "the conversion of the Indians to Roman Catholicism as the replacement of one form of idolatry by another," illustrating

---

53. Ibid., 73.
54. Wilson, *The Church Grows in Canada*, 15.; The term "Huguenots" is not limited to French Protestants in New France but also applies to French Protestants in Europe.

the sharp doctrinal differences between the Huguenots and the French Catholics.[55]

When surveying the history of the Reformation in Europe, the hostility between the Catholics and the Protestants are documented to have been fierce, even deadly, but we do not find the same scale and degree of hostility in Canada (there have been few exceptions), especially after the Edict Nantes in 1598, where "much toleration was extended to the Huguenots" in France.[56] Even then, however, under Catholic influence, the Huguenots were eventually repressed into a minute fraction of New France's population, as scholar Joseph Boucher records:

> The French Protestants in Canada today are not the descendants of those hardy and daring Huguenots who, in the sixteenth and seventeenth centuries, founded the first French settlements on the shores of the St. Lawrence River and the Bay of Fundy... only a few were left when the colony was ceded to Britain.

---

55. Grant, *Moon of Wintertime*, 7-8.
56. Wilson, *The Church Grows in Canada*, 15.

Figure 2: "Champlain on the Ottawa River" by John David Kelly (1917-1958, 20th century). M993.154.59 © McCord Museum.

It appeared that Cartier's beliefs of the Protestant people were shared in spirit amongst the majority of Catholics in New France, in which he described them as "infants of Satan," and "wicked Lutherans, apostates."[57] Champlain, however, was seen as a hero for Protestants during a time of unrest, despite being a Catholic in religion, as scholar David Fischer details:

> Champlain always sought a solution to these problems... He maintained the Catholic Church as an establishment but protected the rights of Protestants to worship. He also worked out a series of flexible compromises that allowed both groups freedom of conscience, but asked them to exercise those rights in ways that did not offend others.[58]

The original plan for France's colonization of the New World was to make all things Catholic, with "Protestantism being excluded" by design, but the French colony on Sable Island represented a change in New France, where openness to Protestantism was made possible by King Henry IV who overturned the "exclusivity of

---

57. Cartier, *The Voyages of Jacques Cartier*, 37.
58. Fischer, *Champlain's Dream*, 380.

an established Catholic faith in the colony" by allowing "Huguenots to hold public office," and to practice their faith freely under the Protestant Chauvin of New France.[59] As the years progressed, the door opened wider for Protestant influence and immigration in the land.

In 1583, Britain commissioned Sir Humphrey Gilbert to "finish what Cabot had started, that is, to claim Newfoundland for England."[60] It was in St. John where he established the organizational structure of Protestant church plants, modeling public worship "according to the Church of England."[61] The growth of British Protestantism in Canada only grew from thereon, with royal orders being issued in 1633 "to hold prayers on Sundays, the Book of Common Prayer being specifically mentioned."[62]

The American historian Noll writes, in regards to the influence of the Protestant reformation on Canada's civilization, that Canada was

---

59. Marcel Trudel, *The Beginnings of New France 1524-1663*, trans. Patricia Claxton (Toronto: The Canadian Publishers, 1973), 60, 65.
60. Wilson, *The Church Grows in Canada*, 18.
61. Ibid.
62. Ibid.

"more observant in religious practice and more orthodox in religious opinion than the United States," which first started "with the creation in Quebec of a full-orbed, organic Catholic society – grounded in the colonial period on the self-sacrificing labors of several religious orders."[63] This claim of Protestant influence, which followed the colonial Catholic faith, is supported by Tom Faulkner of *The Canadian Encyclopedia*, who states that Canada was "shaped decisively by the 3 convictions of Protestantism," listing firstly the "veneration of the Bible," which fostered literacy and popular education; secondly, the "stern standard of morality" derived from God's gift of grace; and thirdly, the "Protestant Ethic," which was to do all things in a spirit of excellence in service to the Lord.[64]

The Major Denominations of Pre-Confederation

Canada emerged from a French Catholicism to a later Protestantism, but there still existed, in

---

63. Noll, *What Happened to Christian Canada?*, 15-17.
64. Tom Faulkner, "Protestantism," The Canadian Encyclopedia, January 31, 2001, accessed June 9, 2016, http://www.thecanadianencyclopedia.ca/en/article/protestantism/.

our nation's history, a diversity within the body of Christ with five major denominations, besides Catholicism, greatly influencing the direction of Canadian society in pre-confederation Canada. Amongst these was the Anglican church, which was first established in the Maritimes in 1758, beginning with Nova Scotia, and later spreading to "Prince Edward Island in 1774, and to Cape Breton in 1785."[65] They earnestly worked towards the "total apparatus of a Christian society," heavily emphasizing a full orbed gospel and the cultivation of a Christian social order rather than a mere privatized faith.[66]

The Presbyterian church was another major denomination, which in its diversity outnumbered the Anglicans. They were first informally introduced by the Huguenots, who could be "classed as a kind of Presbyterian," but later more formally established in Nova Scotia in 1750, by "reformed church immigrants hailing from Holland and Germany," and expanding with

---

65. Wilson, *The Church Grows in Canada*, 21.
66. Grant, *Moon of Wintertime*, 91.

immigrants "from the American colonies prior to the Revolution in 1776."[67]

The Baptists emerged from the southern colonies, with its first representatives arriving into the Maritimes in 1760, filling "the void left by the expulsion of the Acadians in 1755."[68] The first Baptist to have arrived and settled in Canada was Ebenezer Moulton, who founded a church in Horton, Nova Scotia, what is now called "Wolfville Baptist Church,... the oldest Baptist church in Canada."[69] The Baptists were initially a minority compared to the Congregationalists of America, but they quickly grew in number by the end of the century to be a major influence in both the US and Canada.[70]

The Lutherans were also established in the Maritimes around the mid-eighteenth century, coinciding with German immigration, but this was not the first time that they had practiced

---

67. Wilson, *The Church Grows in Canada*, 24.
68. Ibid., 27.
69. Anthony L. Chute, Nathan A. Finn, and Michael A. G. Haykin, *The Baptist Story: From English Sect to Global Movement* (Nashville, TN.: B&H Academic, 2015), 110.
70. Ibid.

their faith on Canadian soil. It was 1619 when a vessel from Denmark arrived on the shores of the Hudson Bay, with approximately sixty onboard, under the leadership of captain Jens Munck. The captain claimed the land as "Nova Dania," what he had hoped would be the future home of his crew. With Munck was the Rev. Rasmus Jensen, a Lutheran minister, who was vital in assisting him with "the first Lutheran attempt at settlement in North America."[71] Unfortunately, their settlement only lasted five months, after which scurvy diminished their number to three. As Wilson writes:

In one of the most heroic ventures in Canadian record Captain Munck, recovered from near death, sailed with his two remaining companions all the way back to Denmark. Behind them lay the body of the first Lutheran minister to die in the New World.[72]

The other major denomination in eighteenth century Canada was Methodism, which began in 1772 with one thousand Yorkshires settling in the "Isthmus of Chignecto" of Newfoundland,

---

71. Wilson, *The Church Grows in Canada*, 30-31.
72. Ibid., 31.

fervently preaching for personal salvation, encouraging the moral "quest for 'the mind of Christ,'" and teaching that "the faith that saves must work in the direction of altered lives and an improved society."[73] The First Nations warmed up to Methodism because they insisted, as Grant writes, that "everyone regardless of race required this radical transformation [which] helped Indians to make the transition with dignity. Essentially they were treated as sinners rather than as inferiors."[74] Although it is not likely that the other denominations were guilty of treating them as "inferiors," aside from isolated incidents, it was Methodism that most emphasized their human dignity and equal rights.

The five significant denominations of the late eighteenth to early nineteenth century Canada, along with the Roman Catholic church, understood the importance of education for its evangelization of culture. It was not only about the gospel's application to the person, they worked towards building high level educational institutions that would teach the gospel's

---

73. Ibid., 33-34.
74. Grant, *Moon of Wintertime*, 90.

application to all areas of life, a full-orbed gospel.[75] As Wilson documented:

> The struggle for public education, both for the common man and for the ministry, was marked by the formation of sectarian academies and colleges by Presbyterians, Baptists and later, Methodists... The circle was [later] complete with every major religious body having one or more educational institutions.[76]

According to Noll, the Christian civilization brought about by the Protestant churches, in partnership with the Catholic minority of Canada, produced:

> Fruitful cooperation between churches and provincial governments in organizing education, social services, and eventually health care; noteworthy syntheses of traditional faith and modern learning that avoided the excesses of both secularization and fundamentalism; deep

---

75. Joe Boot, "Evangelism and Evangelization," Ezra Institute for Contemporary Christianity, October 22, 2015, accessed June 13, 2016, http://www.ezrainstitute.ca/resource-library/interviews/evangelism-and-evangelization/.
76. Wilson, *The Church Grows in Canada*, 38-39.

interpenetration of religious convictions and social values in the outworking of family and community life in many localities.[77]

This was always the vision of the early Protestant missionaries, where "humanitarian concern kept pace with missionary zeal," as reformed Christians sought to "remedy social ills, appealing at first chiefly to individual consciences but increasingly seeking to mould public policy."[78] The church was heavily involved in the cultivation of society, fostering an attitude of acceptance towards national confederation,[79] and responding to the call, as God's people, to instill Christian principles in the public square, preserve national and social stability, and guide the country's conscience.[80] This eventually led to "intradenominational unions," in which the province of Ontario "played a leading

---

77. Noll, *What Happened to Christian Canada?*, 17.
78. Grant, *Moon of Wintertime*, 74.
79. John Webster Grant, *The Church in the Canadian Era*, Updated and Expanded Edition ed. (Vancouver, B.C.: Regent College Publishing, 1988), 24.
80. Neil Semple, *The Lord's Dominion: The History of Canadian Methodism* (Kingston & Montreal: McGills-Queen's University Press, 1996), 427.

part," reflecting the "postmillennial hopes of [Canadian] Protestants" of a Christian Canada from sea to sea, under the sovereign reign of Christ.[81]

In Summary

The introduction of the Christian faith was slow and gradual, beginning first with the raising of the cross by John Cabot in the fifteenth century, and the later demonstration of faith by Jacques Cartier in the sixteenth century. It was under Samuel de Champlain, however, that the Christian religion was successfully expanded amongst the settlers and the First Nations by means of the Récollets, the Jesuits, and the Huguenots in the seventeenth century. The informal partnerships that were formed between Catholics and Protestants, for the advancement of the gospel, were reflective of the growing openness to Protestantism in Canada; and with the growth of the British colonies, the latter became a vast majority in Canada's early history.

---

81. John W. Grant, *A Profusion of Spires: Religion in Nineteenth-Century Ontario* (Toronto: University of Toronto Press, 1988), 228.

From the eighteenth to the nineteenth century, pre-confederation Canada was largely influenced by five Protestant denominations – the Anglicans, the Presbyterians, the Baptists, the Lutherans, and the Methodists – and by Roman Catholicism. As Grant stated, the church believed that Canada ought to be "fashioned into 'God's dominion'… from sea to sea," and their attention was towards "what constituted a righteous [Christian] nation."[82] The Canada of pre-confederation was still split into various colonies, sometimes called British provinces, but their Christian faith united them despite of their distance, contributing towards the development of a Christian civilization, and building towards nationhood in the confederation of 1897.

---

82. Grant, *The Church in the Canadian Era*, 19.

APPENDIX

PEACE TOWER, PARLIAMENT, AND CHRISTIAN CANADA

Canada's heritage as a nation under God is plainly carved on the walls of our Parliamentary buildings. They serve as a rebuke, as well as an encouragement, to all Canadians, that God continues to call His people to covenant faithfulness.

CANADA'S CHRISTIAN HERITAGE has largely been forgotten by the younger generations. Consider, for example, the widespread teaching of Darwinian evolution in our educational institutions,[1] the intolerance of Christian belief

---

1. Steven Chase, 'B.C. MP Quits Conservatives to Defend Views on Evolution', *The Globe and Mail,* March 31, 2015, http://www.theglobeandmail.com/news/politics/bc-mp-quits-conservatives-says-his-christian-worldview-was-suppressed/article23709160/.

in the public square,[2] or the godless (secular) foundation of our law and government.[3] These are all facts of which most young people will say "It has always been so." What can be more tragic, that the youth of our age has no knowledge of our country's founding history, or that they presume that just because things are as they are, then it ought to be so?

From the time of Jacques Cartier, to Sir John A. MacDonald, to the 1960s, there has been a strong interwoven presence of Christianity in Canadian history, up until quite recently. In fact, Canada was always regarded as a "Christian nation,"[4] strongly tied to the Church of England,[5] and wholly devoted to the teaching

---

2. Douglas Farrow, 'Of Secularity and Civil Religion', ed. Douglas Farrow *Recognizing Religion in a Secular Society: Essays in Pluralism, Religion, and Public Policy* (Canada: McGill-Queen's University Press, 2004), 173.

3. Joseph Boot, *The Mission of God: A Manifesto of Hope* (St. Catharines, Ontario: Freedom Press International, 2014), 246-247.

4. John S. Moir, *Christianity in Canada: Historical Essays*, ed. Paul Laverdure (Yorkton, SK: Redeemer's Voice Press, 2002), 1.

5. John Webster Grant, *The Church in the Canadian Era* (Vancouver: Regent College Publishing, 1988), 13.

of God's word.[6] To examine "Christian Canada" would entail volumes upon volumes of writings, something quite lacking besides the works of historians John W. Grant, Eric Crouse, Terrence Murphy, John S. Moir, and few others. There is, however, at the very least, a starting point for fellow Christians to begin their journey of discovery: in our nation's capital.

Inscribed on the Peace Tower and other Parliamentary buildings in Ottawa, are various biblical passages that remind us of the Christian heritage of our nation. This publication is by no means an exhaustive list of the engraved passages, but reviews, as a fraction of the whole, important passages that reflect the grand portrait of our historic national identity. While the biblical vision of our nation may often be neglected, if not completely ignored, by national history curriculums in our public schools, the remnants of what once was can still be reclaimed by a faithful church in our present time. Let

---

6. R.D. Gidney and W.P.J. Millar, 'The Christian Recessional in Ontario's Public Schools', ed. Marguerite Van Die, *Religion and Public Life in Canada: Historical and Comparative Perspectives* (Toronto: University of Toronto Press, 2001), 275.

Figure 3: "He Shall Have Dominion Also From Sea to Sea", inscribed on the Peace Tower in Ottawa, Ontario.

Figure 4: The Peace Tower, Parliament, and the Parliamentary Library. Free image license from Pexels.

us consider the Peace Tower, the buildings of Parliament, and the Memorial Chamber within.

The Peace Tower

The Peace Tower itself bears three primary passages, the most prominent being Psalm 72:8, which is also featured on Canada's coat of arms. The passage reads "May He have dominion from sea to sea, and from the River to the ends of the earth" (ESV), inscribed in Latin on the wall, as "*A Mari usque Ad Mare.*" This is the Psalm which first inspired the Fathers of Confederation to name our nation *The Dominion of Canada*, and despite those who have argued for an initial reference to Israel's first temple era, this passage actually refers to the kingdom of the Messiah.[7] In verses 9-10 the kingdoms of Tarshish, Sheba and Seba are mentioned as under the dominion of this sovereign King, indicating inapplicability to Solomon's reign and suggesting a transcendent rule. The two fundamental components of Psalm 72:8 constitute the absolute sovereignty of God over the entire earth, hence the mention

---

7. Robert Jamieson and A.R. Fausset, *Jamieson, Fausset, and Brown Commentary* (Grand Rapids: Zondervan, 1989), Kindle Edition.

of foreign nations; and that this kingdom and dominion shall be the Lord's. In Daniel 2:44-45 we read the biblical prophecy of God's kingdom establishment, which from a stone a mountain grows, covering the entire earth, echoing Psalm 72:8. It is not a kingdom marked by a particular ethnicity or language, but rather by the unity of multi-ethnic diversity in its creed.

This concept of sovereign rule attributed unto God, not man, is at the root of the celebrations of July 1, *Dominion Day*, which was to recognize God's sovereignty over our nation and all that it entails. This was officially overturned in 1983 in the passing of a private members' bill that proposed changing the name to "Canada Day" with only twelve Members of Parliament present. This formed part of a larger de-Christianization movement,[8] reflecting the change of values and beliefs by Canadian Parliament and its citizens, and the substitution of God with the state as sovereign in the adoption of the

---

8. Michael Wagner, *Leaving God Behind: The Charter of Rights and Canada's Official Rejection of Christianity* (Russell, Ontario: Christian Governance, 2012), 16.

Charter of Rights & Freedoms.[9] It is a statement of a country that sought not submission to God and His law but rather radical autonomy, to be a law unto ourselves, to be our own creators of morality and reality, such as demonstrated by the decriminalization of abortion and the legalization of same-sex marriages, where "life" and "marriage" were redefined.

The other two passages in Scripture are Psalm 72:1 and Proverbs 29:18. The Psalm reads "Give the king your justice, O God, and your righteousness to the royal son!" It is the prayer of the Psalmist for an act that would later take place, the acts and principles of right government given unto the Messiah to rule in perfect justice. It is Christ, not man, who is king over all of God's creation. This follows in line with the Proverb which reads "Where there is no vision, the people perish: but he that keepeth the law, happy is he" (Prov. 29:18, KJV). The Fathers of Confederation had a vision for Canada; it was a Christian nation that rivaled the culture of the United States.[10] To have a vision, as is meant

---

9. Boot, *The Mission of God*, 118-119.
10. Mark A. Noll, *What Happened to Christian*

by the Proverb, is to devote oneself towards the instruction of God's truth through His divinely-inspired Word.[11] For it follows that without the law, without godly instruction, our moral depravity will lead us to our own destruction due to the absence of moral restraints; we will witness the perishing of not only individuals but societies.[12]

The application of this passage is fundamental to understanding the vision of the founding fathers, a nation under God, abiding by the law of God. That is not the vision of today, instead humanism, both religious and secular, has resulted in the decay of truth in the public square and the erosion of our moral foundation. It is the secular humanist who says that "there is no God," that "we are not accountable to God," that "man creates his own meaning, his own morality, and his own freedom." The same in

---

Canada? (Vancouver: Regent College Publishing, 2007), 7-9.

11. Jamieson and Fausset, *Jamieson, Fausset, and Brown Commentary*, Kindle Edition.
12. John Calvin, *Institutes of the Christian Religion*, ed. Henry Beveridge (Peabody, MA: Hendrickson Publishers, 2008), 233-234.

spirit as the religious humanist, though with a religious garb. The age-old vision, as derived from Scripture, is to submit our nation to the sovereignty of the king, Jesus Christ, who rules in perfect justice and with the principles of right government. It is an opposing view to modern understanding, a stark contrast to humanistic religion, but the Peace Tower reminds us of our former Christian identity and the destiny that awaits the wise decisions of godly nations.

Parliament Buildings

A sample of the biblical passages found within the Parliament buildings is Ephesians 6:13 and Psalm 139:8-10. In the Pauline epistle to the Ephesian church, we read "Therefore take up the whole armor of God, that you may be able to withstand in the evil day, and having done all, to stand firm." The people of Ephesus were accustomed to Greek mythology and its tales of their gods providing mortal man with special armor, hence why Paul uses a common illustration to communicate the truth of God in his writings.[13] It is the "taking up of armor" that is

---

13. Jamieson and Fausset, *Jamieson, Fausset, and Brown Commentary*, Kindle Edition.

regarded as a call to arms, to defend and protect God's creation from evil. To neglect the response to evil is morally wrong in itself; we are morally bound by Holy Scripture to respond to evil, just as the western world responded to the cruelty of Nazi Germany in WWII. It is the role of the state to administer justice in all areas of society, to execute justice according to the perfect law of God.

This includes defending against the threat of humanism, the man-centered worldview that perverts justice and righteousness. Just as this passage applies to the preparedness of man individually, it also applies to the spiritual and moral integrity of a nation as a whole. As to the armor, Paul writes of truth, righteousness, peace, faith, salvation and the word of God (divine instruction), all biblical principles that are good and pleasing unto God, qualities that once distinguished our nation's identity.

The Psalmist wrote in Psalm 139:8-10 the following:

> *If I ascend to heaven, you are there!*
> *If I make my bed in Sheol, you are there!*
> *If I take the wings of the morning*

and dwell in the uttermost parts of the sea,
even there your hand shall lead me,
and your right hand shall hold me.

It is the Psalmist's recognition of God's omnipresence and omniscience; He is both everywhere and all-knowing. He knows the deep thoughts of man, the dark sins of the nations, and is present in both private homes and public legislatures. But we not only find recognition of God's attributes, we find a faithful promise, that those who turn to Him will be led by Him, and that in His nearness He also sustains us. It was a declaration of dependence upon God, a demonstration of humility, a forgotten devotion that has been substituted with the idol of self and independence.

Memorial Chamber

In the memorial chamber of Parliament we find references to Jeremiah 23:5, which reads "… execute judgment and justice in the earth" and Nahum 1:7, "The LORD is good, a stronghold in the day of trouble; he knows those who take refuge in him." The Messiah king does not just reign over a spiritual kingdom, but righteously reigns over the entire earth (Jer. 3:17, 18). The mistaken belief that the kingdom of God is merely spiritual and does not incorporate the physical world is damaging to the work of the church. This was the vision of our forefathers, that Christ would execute "judgment and justice." Perhaps the question may be asked about the injustices in our own legal history, such as the court decisions to allow and even publicly fund the massacre of the unborn, but what we ought to be reminded of is that, if Christ is sovereign, which He is, He will execute justice even if the state fails to fulfill its role.

The legal system was not meant to replace the judgment of God, it was meant to uphold the law of God, and whatever judgment is given by the courts, Christ will still administer the final judgment. A guilty man convicted of murder will not escape the judgment of God after serving twenty-five years in prison; it is Christ who will "judge the living and the dead" (2 Tim. 4:1). Although the passage of Jeremiah affirms the sovereignty of God and His righteousness and judgment, Nahum assures us of the safety and refuge available in Christ. A man can escape the wrath of God by repenting of his sin and turning to Jesus Christ; likewise, a nation can escape the judgment of God by turning to the King on His throne, who has conquered both sin and death. These are messages of both hope and judgment, the good news of God and the penalty for breaking His perfect law.

Concluding Remarks

These inscribed biblical passages on the Peace Tower and Parliamentary buildings are merely scratching the surface of Canada's Christian heritage; they provide a glimpse of our original national vision and the future hope of restoring a nation under God. The vaults of Canadian history are filled with fundamental Christian belief, but our secularized society has tirelessly worked to bury that fact, to eliminate all such traces of the past. To study the spiritual roots of our nation, and how it has poured out into other areas of life and society, is a worthy pursuit recommended for all Canadian Christians. Most importantly, it is a long-neglected work of the church, a vital task in reclaiming its evangelistic vigor and zeal for the glorification of God in the public square. Such a task can only be done by the understanding of Canadian church history, and by embracing the *missio dei*, the mission of God, as outlined by the Holy Scriptures (Matt. 28:18-19).

It ought to be known that there was such a thing as a "Christian Canada", however you might choose to define it, and there is hope, in God's providence, for a renewed conversion of our nation. It only follows that if our faith is in a sovereign and righteous God, infinite in power and strength, with a gospel that can transform minds and hearts, then we should expect the church to adopt a victorious outlook toward history, in which the "gates of hell shall not prevail" (Matt. 16:18), and where man can not only be saved in Jesus Christ (John 3:16) but be redeemed and renewed (John 3:3).

ABOUT THE AUTHOR

STEVEN R. MARTINS is founding director of the Cántaro Institute and founding pastor of Sevilla Chapel in St. Catharines, ON. He has worked in the fields of missional apologetics and church leadership for over ten years and has spoken at numerous conferences, churches, and University student events. He has also contributed articles to *Coalición por el Evangelio* (TGC in Spanish) and the *Siglo XXI* journal of Editorial CLIR. Steven holds a Master's degree *summa cum laude* in Theological Studies with a focus on Christian apologetics from Veritas International University (Santa Ana, CA., USA) and a Bachelor of Human Resource Management from York University (Toronto, ON., Canada). Steven is married to Cindy and they live in Lincoln, Ontario, with their four children.

www.ingramcontent.com/pod-product-compliance
Lightning Source LLC
Chambersburg PA
CBHW040109120526
44589CB00040B/2827